WITHDR
FEB 201

D1371124

LAKE VILLA DISTRICT LIBRARY

3 1981 00604 9674

Connecting Cultures Through Family and Food

The Japanese Family Table

by Mari Rich

Connecting Cultures Through Family and Food

The Japanese Family Table

By Mari Rich

MASON CREST

Lake Villa District Library
Lake Villa, Illinois 60046
(847) 356-7711

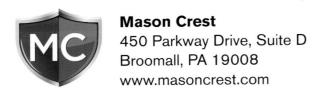

Mason Crest
450 Parkway Drive, Suite D
Broomall, PA 19008
www.masoncrest.com

© 2019 by Mason Crest, an imprint of National Highlights, Inc.

All rights reserved. No part of this publication may be reproduced or transmitted in any form or by any means, electronic or mechanical, including photocopying, recording, taping, or any information storage and retrieval system, without permission in writing from the publisher.

Printed and bound in the United States of America.

First printing
9 8 7 6 5 4 3 2 1

Series ISBN: 978-1-4222-4041-0
Hardback ISBN: 978-1-4222-4047-2
EBook ISBN: 978-1-4222-7745-4

Produced by Shoreline Publishing Group LLC
Santa Barbara, California
Editorial Director: James Buckley Jr.
Designer: Tom Carling
Production: Patty Kelley
www.shorelinepublishing.com
Front cover: Tetra Images/Alamy Stock Photo (top); Natalia Lisovskaya/Dreamstime.com

Library of Congress Cataloging-in-Publication Data
Names: Rich, Mari, author. Title: The Japanese family table / by Mari Rich.
Description: Broomall, PA : Mason Crest, 2018. | Series: Connecting cultures through family and food | Includes index.
Identifiers: LCCN 2018001653| ISBN 9781422240472 (hardback) | ISBN 9781422240410 (series) | ISBN 9781422277454 (ebook)
Subjects: LCSH: Food habits--Japan--Juvenile literature. | Japanese Americans--Social life and customs--Juvenile literature.
Classification: LCC GT2853.J3 R53 2018 | DDC 394.1/20952--dc23 LC record available at https://lccn.loc.gov/2018001653

QR Codes disclaimer:

You may gain access to certain third party content ("Third-Party Sites") by scanning and using the QR Codes that appear in this publication (the "QR Codes"). We do not operate or control in any respect any information, products, or services on such Third-Party Sites linked to by us via the QR Codes included in this publication, and we assume no responsibility for any materials you may access using the QR Codes. Your use of the QR Codes may be subject to terms, limitations, or restrictions set forth in the applicable terms of use or otherwise established by the owners of the Third-Party Sites. Our linking to such Third-Party Sites via the QR Codes does not imply an endorsement or sponsorship of such Third-Party Sites, or the information, products, or services offered on or through the Third- Party Sites, nor does it imply an endorsement or sponsorship of this publication by the owners of such Third-Party Sites.

Contents

KEY ICONS TO LOOK FOR

Words to Understand: These words with their easy-to-understand definitions will increase the reader's understanding of the text, while building vocabulary skills.

Sidebars: This boxed material within the main text allows readers to build knowledge, gain insights, explore possibilities, and broaden their perspectives by weaving together additional information to provide realistic and holistic perspectives.

Educational Videos: Readers can view videos by scanning our QR codes, providing them with additional educational content to supplement the text. Examples include news coverage, moments in history, speeches, iconic moments, and much more!

Text-Dependent Questions: These questions send the reader back to the text for more careful attention to the evidence presented here.

Research Projects: Readers are pointed toward areas of further inquiry connected to each chapter. Suggestions are provided for projects that encourage deeper research and analysis.

Series Glossary of Key Terms: This back-of-the-book glossary contains terminology used throughout this series. Words found here increase the reader's ability to read and comprehend higher-level books and articles in this field.

Introduction

Japan is a nation of islands located off the east coast of Asia. It stretches for some 1,500 miles (2414 km) through the North Pacific Ocean and consists of four main islands—Hokkaido, Honshu, Shikoku, and Kyushu—along with several smaller islands. The capital, Tokyo, located on Honshu, is now one of the world's most densely populated cities, but Japan also has lush forests, towering mountains, and sparkling lakes.

All that natural beauty remained unknown to Westerners for hundreds of years. In the 1630s, Japan's leaders had begun worrying about the dangers of outside influences and the possibility that a European country would try to colonize them. They enacted an official policy limiting contact with the rest of the world. The edict decreed that Japanese ships were forbidden to sail to foreign countries and that no Japanese citizen could attempt to go abroad, on penalty of death.

Then, in 1853, US Navy Commodore Matthew Perry sailed gunships into Tokyo harbor and forced trade routes to reopen. Suddenly, the people of Japan, who had been isolated for centuries, learned of new and different cultures.

A few years later, when an emperor once again took control after centuries of rule by the *shogun* (military leader)—a turn of events called the Meiji Restoration—the country underwent a period of great social and economic transformation. Cities grew, farmers were forced to leave their land, and workers were left

unemployed or underpaid because of foreign competition.

Some Japanese people started to think they might have a chance at a better life if they left their homeland.

Today, about 2.6 million people of Japanese descent live outside Japan, according to the Association of Nikkei and Japanese Abroad. About 100,000 can be found in the Philippines (with some of these descended from Japanese Catholics who fled in the 17th century to avoid religious persecution). Other small segments have settled in the United Kingdom (mainly for the educational opportunities presented by the universities in Oxford and Cambridge) and Peru.

More than a million have chosen to settle in Brazil, and the two countries share a deep history of cultural and economic exchange. Because of those ties, Brazilians also comprise the largest non-Asian ethnic group living in Japan. Each year, there are several Japanese festivals held in Brazil, and the Brazilian Asakusa Samba Carnival is one of the biggest summer festivals in Tokyo. In Peru, a man of Japanese descent named Alberto Fujimori rose to become president.

Another large group is in the United States, with major communities in New York City, California, Washington State, and Oregon. Japanese people have endured prejudice and hardship in America—especially during World War II, when the United States and Japan fought on opposite sides—but they have survived and thrived despite those circumstances.

Though Japanese immigration numbers are not as high as some other groups, those who come have found places to live together.

Japanese restaurants are familiar sights in most Western cities.

Even Americans who live in communities with few people of Japanese descent are probably familiar with certain aspects of that country's culture, especially its food. According to some estimates there are now more than 9,000 Japanese restaurants across the United States—from inexpensive chicken-teriyaki places in mall food courts to fine dining establishments where a meal of sushi prepared by a famed chef can cost hundreds of dollars.

Japanese immigrants haven't just introduced delicious new foods to the countries in which they've settled, however. They've helped make their new homes more diverse and interesting places.

Getting Here

In the 1880s, Hawaii was not yet a US state. Still, much of its economy was controlled by powerful US-based businesses, including many large fruit and sugar plantations. The managers of the plantations often sent agents to Japan to recruit young men to come work there. Because of economic and social upheaval in their own country, many agreed to immigrate, signing labor contracts that strongly favored the business owners.

Life on the plantations could be hard. The work day was long and toiling in the hot sun was exhausting. The housing provided by the companies was often cramped and dirty. Still, Japanese immigrants persevered, and by 1898, when Hawaii became a US territory, there were almost 60,000 Japanese living on the Hawaiian Islands.

Words to Understand

mainland a continent or the main part of a continent, rather than an offshore island or peninsula

prefecture in Japan, the word for a political division much like a state

proxy a person who has authority to act for another

This statue in Hawaii honors Japanese migrant farmers who came to the islands in the 1800s to work on sugar and pineapple plantations.

11

Once Hawaii was a territory, unfair long-term labor contracts, like the ones most immigrants had signed, became illegal. Some workers ultimately returned to Japan, but others took the opportunity to move to the West Coast of the United States. In the years directly after 1908, when a massive labor strike failed to result in higher wages or better working conditions, some 40,000 laborers left Hawaii for California and the surrounding areas. This was the first large group of Japanese immigrants on the US **mainland**.

The city of San Francisco has a strong Japanese connection. This gate is the entrance to a large garden in Japantown there.

Early Life on the Mainland

It was easy for Japanese workers to find jobs on the mainland. They worked building railroads, logging, and mining. Because many had grown up on farms in Japan or had gotten used to farm labor in Hawaii, some worked in California's lush fields and dreamed of owning land of their own one day.

In whatever industry they chose, the Japanese quickly earned a reputation for being fast and efficient workers. They were also good at saving money and many were eventually able to realize their dreams of buying land or businesses of their own. Sisters, daughters, and wives who had remained back in Japan were able to join them.

Meanwhile, single men were faced with the challenge of finding Japanese wives of their own. With relatively few women on the mainland to choose from, many turned to their homeland to broaden the search. Men who remained in Hawaii faced the same dilemma.

Pretty as a Picture

From 1908 to 1924, more than 20,000 women came from Japan to America or the Hawaiian Islands to become "picture brides." Japan had a long tradition of *omiai*, or arranged marriages, meaning that a woman's parents picked the man she would marry. Picture brides were an extension of this practice, with prospective brides and grooms agreeing to marry before even meeting, simply on the basis of a photo. According to some genealogists, most Japanese Americans can trace their ancestry back to a picture bride.

Miyoshi Yokota Okamura, a picture bride whose family has preserved her history for the Angel Island Immigration Station Foundation, was born in the Kochi **prefecture** of Japan in 1894. As a schoolgirl she learned the concept of *ryosai kenbo* ("good wife, wise mother") and was raised to obey her parents without question. When a *nakkodo* (a go-between or matchmaker) explained to her family that Kameji Okamura, who lived on the West Coast of America, was searching for a Japanese bride, they shared her photo with him and a match was made.

A wedding ceremony was held in Japan, with a **proxy** standing in for the groom, and Miyoshi began making plans to sail with other picture brides aboard a California-bound ship. Even though she had no say in

Japanese picture brides were chosen by husbands to join them in the West.

her marriage, she was still excited to be embarking on an adventure in America.

Not every picture bride was as happy as Miyoshi. The Angel Island Immigration Station Foundation has collected many stories of women who were devastated at being forced to leave home and miserable to be married to men they had not chosen. Those who were sent to meet men in Hawaii were forced to endure the same harsh work conditions as their new husbands, with the added burden of cooking and cleaning when they returned from the fields.

Aboard the ship, Miyoshi used a knife and fork and ate American food for the first time. It was not a huge success: She mistakenly gulped down a large lump of butter, thinking it was an egg yolk. Also, she found it disgusting to be served meat still on the bone, rather than sliced thinly and served in small portions, as she was accustomed.

A picture bride's story

When her ship docked, she was carefully screened at the immigration station on Angel Island, in San Francisco Bay. Once it was determined that she was healthy, authorities allowed Kameji to pick her up, and the pair wed (in person this time) soon after.

Sakura Kumamoto came to the United States from Japan 10 years ago. While she expected to remain just one year to learn English, she fell in love with an American man named Brian, and married him. While her experience was very different from that of Miyoshi several decades earlier, they had one thing in common. Neither liked American food at first.

By the 2000s, Japanese people had become a vital part of American culture, contributing in many fields.

"I had a sandwich and couldn't even tell whether it was turkey or ham," Sakura recalls. "All I could taste was salt!" Even the American desserts her husband thought she might like caused her to grimace, so excessively sweet did they taste to her.

Text-Dependent Questions:

1. What event important to this story happened in 1898?

2. How did the first Japanese immigrants to the US mainland earn a living?

3. What is the concept of *ryosai kenbo*?

Research Project:

Angel Island is sometimes called the Ellis Island of the West. Why do you think that is? Look at the website of the Angel Island Immigration Station Foundation, a nonprofit historical preservation group, and write down five interesting facts about it.

SNACKS AND STREET FOOD

In Japan, there is a vibrant culture surrounding snacks and drinks. Visiting an *izakaya*, which is similar to a tapas bar in Spain or a pub in Britain, is an enjoyable and important part of social life for many people.

There are several types of *izakaya* throughout Japan. Some are formal; these require patrons to remove their shoes and sit on woven *tatami* mats on the floor. Others, known as *akachochin*, after the red lanterns that typically hang in their entryways, are more informal and cost less. Just as in the United States, some establishments are part of big, national chains. There are said to be at least 80,000 *izakaya* in Japan.

Sake, an alcoholic beverage made from fermented rice, has been brewed for hundreds of years. Food historians have found mentions of sake (pronounced SAH-kee) in books from the third century. Sake was brewed at the imperial court and drunk by the emperor or used for ceremonial purposes. By the middle ages, it was being brewed at Shinto shrines and Buddhist temples as well. Today, large breweries use computer-controlled equipment to produce sake on a massive scale, and it remains one of the drinks most associated with Japan. It is traditionally served warm, in small, rounded cups.

Before more modern methods of fermentation were discovered in about the eighth century, sake was produced by chewing on raw grains of rice and then spitting into vats. The enzymes in the human saliva, along with natural yeast, would help the rice ferment into an alcoholic beverage. This was known as kuchikami-zake, or "mouth-chewed sake."

Note: Alcoholic beverages are only consumed by adults here and in Japan.

Another highly popular drink at any izakaya is shochu, a strong distilled beverage made from rice, barley, or buckwheat. (Sometimes sweet potatoes figure in the recipe.) It is informally (and inaccurately) called "Japanese vodka" and is usually consumed mixed with water because it is so strong.

SNACK TIME!

Drinks are always accompanied by some type of food in Japan. Many of these are referred to as *sakana*, which comes from combining *saka* (sake) and *na* (food). Sometimes the word *otsumami* (snacks or finger food) is used instead. (The word *otsumami* comes from the verb *tsumamu*, meaning "to grab.")

Among the most popular snacks are those based on types of seafood. To make ika ten, *a thin piece of squid is coated in a thin batter, fried, and sprinkled with salt, red chili pepper, or other seasonings. Fans say it has an interesting texture—crunchy and chewy at the same time.*

Squid is also used to make saki ika; *it's dried and shredded into thin pieces and seasoned. Some people compare it to beef jerky.* Ika kun *is another popular variation of dried squid. It takes the form of small rings (like that seen on Italian menus as calamari).* Kun *is an affectionate Japanese term for a young child, and the implication seems to be that the rings are small and cute.*

Other popular seafood snacks include saba heshiko nukazuke *(pickled mackerel),* tatami iwashi *(a flat "cracker" made of dried baby sardines),* karashi mentaiko *(cod roe with salt and chili powder),* negitoro *(chopped raw tuna),* and momiji zuke *(salmon and its roe in sweet soy sauce). (Roe are fish eggs, which are popular in many countries. Think of caviar.)*

Another popular snack made with chicken is yakitori, *skewers of chicken or chewy chicken cartilage that have been marinated and grilled. Even vegetables get into the act at snack time: pickled daikon (radish) and edamame (steamed or boiled young soybeans) are salty enough to ensure that the patrons at an izakaya work up a thirst.*

Settling In

ike many Japanese men of his era, Kameji earned a living as a farmer. Early arrivals to the mainland formed small communities in towns along the West Coast, and he took his new bride to the Seattle area until he could save up enough money to buy land and a home of his own. Other Japanese immigrants worked in mines, **canneries**, or lumber mills, and some opened stores and boarding houses.

By 1920 Japanese-born farmers owned an estimated 450,000 acres of land in California and were responsible for more than 10 percent of the state's crop revenue. Even though they were generally hardworking and polite, Japanese

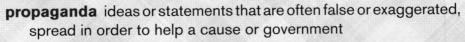

Words to Understand

canneries   factories where food is canned

propaganda ideas or statements that are often false or exaggerated, spread in order to help a cause or government

quota system   in this case, a plan that limits the number of a certain kind of people who can immigrate in a country

xenophobic showing a dislike of or prejudice against people from other countries

This 1930s farmer in California was part of a growing tradition of Japanese coming to that state to take advantage of good land and great weather.

immigrants were often met with prejudice. **Propaganda** was spread that Japanese men were enemies of the average American laborer and a menace to American women.

The Immigration Act of 1924 imposed severe restrictions that ended Japanese immigration to America for many years. The Immigration Act, also known as the Johnson-Reed Act, called for a harsh **quota system** that provided visas to a minuscule number of prospective immigrants and *completely* excluded those from Asia.

By the time the **xenophobic** and exclusionary legislation took effect, however, Kameji and Miyoshi had established a good life for themselves. It had not been easy at first. Miyoshi had given up the comfortable kimonos and wooden sandals she was used to in exchange for unfamiliar

Japanese women find a time and place to wear traditional dress.

skirts, dresses, and shoes. She didn't speak English and had a hard time communicating in stores not run by other Japanese immigrants. Much of the food available locally was unfamiliar to her, and even cleaning her house required different skills—mopping, for example—than were necessary back in her native land. (Because no one in Japan wore shoes in the house, floors were rarely mopped.) To help her settle in, Kameji hired a teacher to help her with her English and a housekeeper to help her adjust to her new homemaking duties. Despite those expenses, he had soon saved enough to buy land in Idaho, where he established a large garden center.

Sakura had some of the same problems when she first arrived in the United States to study. "I longed to eat rice and fish like I was used to," she explains. "But as a student, I didn't have much money, and good-quality seafood was so expensive." She noticed, however, that small takeout places scattered throughout the city offered relatively low-cost Chinese food. It included rice and small bits of meat or fish stir-fried with vegetables, and it was closer to the dishes she craved than inexpensive Western meals like burgers or pizza. "That didn't work out too well though," she admitted. "Americanized Chinese food was heavier and greasier than I expected, and I never felt well after eating it."

A New Generation

The legislators who passed the Immigration Act of 1924 might have crushed the dreams of many of those who sought to make new lives in America, but they could not stop those already here from having children. Miyoshi and Kameji had a total of seven children—two boys and five girls. By 1930, half of the people of Japanese descent in the United

States had been born here. These were the Nisei—the children of the original Japanese immigrants, known as the Issei. Because they were born here, the Nisei were automatically considered American citizens, and they straddled two worlds: eating traditional Japanese food at home with their parents and American meals while out with their friends, speaking Japanese at home and English at school, and being drawn to Christianity instead of Buddhism.

Generations

Issei first-generation immigrants; those who came before Japanese immigration to America ceased because of the Immigration Act of 1924. Most Issei were middle-aged or older during World War II.

Nisei the American-born children of the Issei.

Sansei the third generation (meaning the grandchildren of the Issei and children of the Nisei).

Yonsei fourth-generation Japanese Americans.

Shin-Issei the prefix *shin* means "new," and this term is sometimes used to describe the immigrants who came from Japan after the end of World War II.

A Culture Clash over Lunch

Japanese people often tote their lunches in bento boxes, containers with individual compartments for serving various foods. The custom dates back to the 12th century, when rice was cooked and then stored in lacquer boxes to eat later. (The word bento means "convenient.") A typical bento box lunch contains rice, fish or meat, hardboiled eggs, vegetables or salad, pickled foods, and sometimes fruit. Japanese convenience stores and groceries sell premade bento lunches, but many parents put a lot of time and thought into making attractive and appealing meals for their children. Thanks to the internet and instructional YouTube videos, the custom has even spread to parents in America.

Kyaraben refers to a style of bento that features food decorated to look like people, cartoon characters, animals, plants, and anything else the cook can dream up. Stores sell special supplies, like miniature cookie cutters and fancy picks, to inspire the lunch makers to new heights of imagination. There are even national contests sponsored by big Japanese companies, like Sanrio, that offer prizes for the cutest, most elaborate *kyaraben* creations.

Linda Furiya remembers feeling conflicted during lunch hour every day of the first grade. She is a writer who belongs to the Nisei generation. Her parents' marriage had been arranged by a go-between, and the two met for the first time at the airport, when her mother arrived in the

Making a bento box lunch

United States. ("The Western style of dating was as foreign to them as eating a bowl of corn flakes with milk for breakfast," the writer recalled in her memoir, *Bento Box in the Heartland*. "Every morning Dad ate a bowl of leftover warmed-up rice and one raw beaten egg with a little soy sauce drizzled over it, and Mom had a bowl of miso soup with rice.")

The young Linda desperately wanted to have bologna and cheese sandwiches like her friends, but her mother insisted on packing bento boxes of *onigiri*, neat little balls of rice filled with chunks of fish or pickled plum, which she loved but which she saw as "a glaring reminder of the

Onigiri *is a traditional Japanese snack. Rice is packed or rolled into balls or triangular shapes. Inside might be a bit of fish or plum.*

ethnic differences between my peers and me." She spent the entire year eating the fruit from her bento while in the school cafeteria and then ducking into a bathroom stall to wolf down the delicious *onigiri* in secret.

There are some people who say that the process of making fancy bento boxes has become too competitive and stressful, with parents getting up early in the morning to spend hours packing lunches that will be eaten in minutes and perhaps not even appreciated.

Text-Dependent Questions:

1. Who are the Nisei?

2. Why was Miyoshi unfamiliar with the chore of mopping floors?

3. What is another name for the Immigration Act of 1924?

Research Project:

The contents of a bento box are limited only by the cook's imagination. Search for photos of some appealing bento lunches. Plan one yourself and make a shopping list of the food and supplies you'd need to make it.

SOUP AND SALADS

It's a little bit inaccurate to talk about "courses" when discussing Japanese cuisine. Although a typical American meal might start out with soup or salad, progress through the main course, and end with dessert, in Japan things are done differently. A typical Japanese meal served at home takes the form of a single course, with many dishes served at the same time. (Dessert is still served separately, however.)

Rice is so important in Japanese cuisine that gohan, *a word that means "rice," has come to mean "meal" itself— even when the meal being referred to is a Western-style one containing no rice at all, like a hamburger or spaghetti.*

Even though soup might not be considered a separate first course, it is usually an important part of a Japanese gohan. *The most common type of soup is cooked with miso paste. Miso paste is made by fermenting soybeans with salt and a fungus called koji. (The scientific name for koji is Aspergillus oryzae.)*

Food experts estimate that four-fifths of all the miso produced in Japan goes into soup. About three-quarters of all Japanese people eat soup at least once a day.

Before taking a bite of food or sip of soup, Japanese people say itadakimasu, *which roughly translates as* "I receive this food." *That is considered a polite way to thank the person who worked to prepare the meal.*

After eating, thanks are expressed again by saying, gochiso sama deshita, *which means,* "That was quite a feast!"

To make miso soup, the miso paste is stirred into a clear broth known as dashi. (The miso makes the broth cloudy.) Dashi can be made by boiling a highly flavorful or salty ingredient, like dried shitake mushrooms or kelp for vegetarian versions, or dried baby sardines or bonito (the Japanese name for dried skipjack tuna) for those who like fish.

As a change of pace, sometimes soup is made by leaving out the miso and cooking small bits of vegetables, seafood, or meat in the clear dashi. A good cook will choose the ingredients carefully, depending on what is in season and what mixture will strike the right balance of flavors, textures, and even colors. Mushrooms, potatoes, tofu, seaweed, onions, shrimp, fish, clams, and daikon radish are all popular ingredients to serve in dashi.

In Japan, soups are usually sipped from small, rimless bowls instead of eaten with spoons. If there are solid ingredients, they are plucked from the bowl and eaten with chopsticks. Sometimes in Japan soup is even eaten for breakfast, along with rice. It's a good thing it's so healthy! Miso and dashi are naturally low in calories and high in protein. Some scientists think that eating lots of miso soup might even protect against certain forms of cancer.

SOUP AND SALADS

If you've ever eaten in a Japanese restaurant, you were probably served a green salad with a delicious orange dressing filled with grated carrots and ginger. While there is some question about the authenticity of the recipe, since it was popularized by big Japanese steakhouses catering to Westerners, a typical Japanese meal does sometimes include fresh-lettuce salads like those eaten in the United States. But salads in Japan can also mean much more than a few tossed greens.

Namasu (pictured) is made by shredding a variety of raw vegetables and dressing them with rice vinegar, sugar, and salt.

Another category of salad is sunomono, *a term including foods pickled in vinegar. Thinly sliced cucumber* sunomono *is a favorite, particularly in the summer.*

In goma-ae, the vegetables are blanched, doused with sesame dressing, and served chilled or at room temperature.

Most hijiki is sold dried (pictured) and must be reconstituted (restored to its original state) with water.

Horensou no goma-ae, *made with fresh spinach, is a savory Japanese twist on American spinach salad. Other salads are made with* hijiki, *a wild seaweed found on Japan's rocky coastlines. High in vitamins and minerals, it has been eaten in Japan for hundreds of years.*

Potato salad might seem like an all-American dish, but it's also beloved in Japan, thanks to the popularity of mayonnaise there.

Japanese potato salad often includes ingredients we might consider unusual; instead of the diced celery and onion many American cooks include, it might feature finely diced ham or cucumbers, for example.

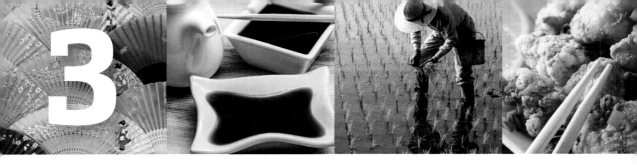

3

Connecting

In Pocatello, Idaho, where they had established their garden center, Miyoshi, Kameji, and their children were popular with their neighbors. He helped organize the Pocatello Japanese Association, was an active member of the Japanese Farmers' Association, and arranged for a nearby cemetery to set aside a section specifically for Japanese families. While their Japanese heritage remained very important to them, they became fully **integrated** into life in Pocatello, participating in local parades and handing out Christmas gifts to the garden center's customers. Miyoshi sometimes gave cabbages she had grown to her German neighbor, who returned the favor with batches of homemade sauerkraut.

Many Japanese immigrants and their growing Japanese American families felt exactly the same way—proud of their place in American society but equally proud

Words to Understand

compensation money given to make up for loss, injury, or suffering
creed a formal statement of beliefs
integrated having parts or aspects that are linked or coordinated

Japanese people have brought their traditions of music, dress, drama, and literature to America and to other countries where they have moved.

of their Japanese heritage. There was even a **creed** recited at the meetings of the Japanese American Citizens League (JACL), a well-known and influential organization, that stated: "I am proud that I am an American citizen of Japanese ancestry, for my very background makes me appreciate more fully the wonderful advantages of this nation."

But trouble was on the horizon.

A Devastating Turn of Events

On December 7, 1941, Japan—intent upon becoming the dominant power in East Asia—sent its navy to attack the US fleet at Pearl Harbor, Hawaii. The United States was plunged into World War II, and suddenly, anyone of Japanese descent became a person of suspicion—even the Nisei who had lived in America their whole lives.

American newspapers published stories that the Japanese were spies and enemy agents, and within a week thousands of prominent Japanese businessmen, writers, teachers, and others had been arrested on the grounds that they were risks to American security. Especially on the West Coast, Japanese people were fired from their jobs and physically attacked in public.

In February of 1942, President Franklin D. Roosevelt signed an order directing the US military to force Japanese people from their homes in "military areas" near the West Coast and relocate them to "internment camps"—basically, prison camps. In one of the most shameful periods in American history, Japanese residents were given one week to register with authorities, gather whatever possessions they could carry, sell their houses and businesses, and report for relocation to their assigned camp.

By the end of the war in 1945, some 125,000 people, many of them children, had been subject to that horrendous treatment, with most sent to harsh barbed-wire-enclosed facilities in the swamplands of Arkansas; deserts of Utah, Arizona, and Colorado; and other forbidding places.

Trying to Return to Normal

The period after World War II was a difficult one for everyone involved. The Issei had lost their homes, businesses, and farms and had to struggle for decades to win even partial **compensation** for those hard-earned assets. It was not until 1980, when Congress established the Commission on Wartime Relocation and Internment of Civilians, that the matter was officially addressed. Finally, in 1988, President Ronald Reagan signed a bill

These Japanese American families are loading their possessions after being forced from their homes during World War II.

that called for paying $20,000 to each surviving Japanese American person who had been placed in an internment camp and providing tuition funds for their children. The Nisei struggled along with their parents, helping to rebuild lost businesses, dealing with lingering prejudice, and learning to take their places as young leaders of the Japanese American community.

There was yet another group struggling to adapt in America during the post-war years: the tens of thousands of young Japanese women who had married American soldiers during the war and subsequently joined them in cities and towns across the United States. War brides, as they were known, went through the same adjustments as earlier immigrants had—with the added burden of being the only Japanese person in their new families and facing the censure of those who were angry that the

Allied soldiers, such as these from Australia, met and married many Japanese women during the years after World War II ended.

returning soldiers had brought home "the enemy."

In 1952, the US government implemented the McCarran-Walter Act, which amended the 1924 Immigration Act, made immigration from Japan legal again, and finally allowed the Issei to become official US citizens (a process known as naturalization).

The Shin-Issei and Changing Tastes

After the McCarran-Walter Act came into effect, a new generation of immigrants, sometimes called the Shin-Issei, began arriving from Japan.

One of these was Hiroaki "Rocky" Aoki, whose father had owned a small coffee shop in Tokyo. After finishing college in Japan, Rocky came

Teriyaki Time

In 1976, Toshihiro Kasahara, a Japanese-born businessman, opened Toshi's Teriyaki Restaurant in Seattle, Washington. Local diners loved the sweet mixture of soy sauce and rice wine used to marinade the meat before grilling, and the style took off. There are now more than 80 Seattle restaurants with "teriyaki" in their name, including one straightforwardly called I Love Teriyaki.

Most dishes served in these establishments have little in common with traditional teriyaki, however; their cooks, who are often not even from Japan, sweeten their concoctions with brown sugar or pineapple juice and add ingredients like peanut butter or coconut.

to the United States to pursue his dream of opening the first teppanyaki restaurant in America. Teppanyaki is a cooking style in which the food is grilled on a hot, flat surface; knowing how much Americans loved barbecuing, he reasoned that they would also enjoy teppanyaki. He earned money upon his arrival by selling ice cream on the streets of New York City, and thanks in part to his idea of decorating the treats with colorful miniature umbrellas made out of paper, he had soon saved up enough to launch his first restaurant. Benihana, named after Aoki's parents' coffee shop, opened in midtown Manhattan in 1964 and became wildly popular. It is now a chain with more than 70 restaurants across America, and scores

If you've been to a Benihana or similar restaurant, you'll recognize this hot grill used to cook Japanese food right at your table.

of other teppanyaki restaurants have also opened with great success. Many of these follow Benihana's practice of hiring teppanyaki chefs who also double as entertainers—juggling their knives, flipping bits of food into patrons' mouths from their stations behind the grill, and stacking raw onion rings into flaming volcanoes.

Teppanyaki is popular with Americans partly because it features large portions of meat. While many Japanese people dismiss restaurants like Benihana as wholly inauthentic, there is a growing trend among Japanese Americans to eat more meat. Even the Issei were not immune to that phenomenon. When Miyoshi had a chance to visit Japan after living in America for four decades, she found that she was not used to eating fish at every meal, as her parents still did. She craved meat so badly that her mother finally agreed to slaughter one of the chickens she had been keeping to lay eggs.

The Benihana story

A Matter of Health

Eating a traditional diet, Japanese women live an average of 87 years, while men live about 80 years. According to a study published in a Japanese medical journal, people who followed the official Japanese governmental dietary guidelines had a 15 percent lower mortality rate. However, eating a lot of meat and processed foods, as in a more Westernized

Karaage

If you don't like seafood, don't worry. There are plenty of other *sakana* you might enjoy trying. To make *karaage*, small chunks of chicken are marinated, lightly coated in wheat flour or potato starch, and deep fried. Japanese people like to dip their *karaage* in some type of sauce (much like Americans dip their chicken nuggets in honey-mustard or barbecue sauce). Many of the most popular dips are made with mayonnaise—specifically Kewpie brand, which has been sold in Japan since 1925 and which contains twice as much egg yolk as American mayonnaise.

diet, can have a bad effect on health. Japanese people living in the West are prone to increasing rates of obesity, higher cholesterol levels, more cases of diabetes, and greater cancer risks.

On the other hand, health-conscious Westerners who eat more Japanese food see the benefits of a lighter diet filled with more seafood and vegetables. This phenomenon has lead to a massive increase in the popularity of sushi (See page 48). Social scientists who study food trends say that after Italian, Chinese, and Mexican, Japanese food is one of the most popular ethnic cuisines in the United States.

Smart Japanese chefs introduced American diners to sushi in the form of California rolls, which use avocado instead of raw fish, and soon Americans were willing to try the real thing. Tim Zagat, who co-founded the Zagat Restaurant Survey, remembers that in the 1990 edition of his guidebook there were ratings of just 34 popular Japanese restaurants across the country; there are currently hundreds. "The idea of eating raw fish? Most people thought that would be a fraternity prank," he told one journalist. "Now there's a sushi bar on every corner." Zagat may have been exaggerating, but Japanese restaurants can now be found in almost every sizeable city and town.

Declining J-Towns

Many immigrants to the United States settled in still-thriving ethnic enclaves—think of the bustling Chinatowns you can visit in most large cities. It is much more unusual, however, to find Japantowns (or J-Towns, as they are sometimes called).

When the Issei were first getting settled on the West Coast, they formed more than 40 different J-Towns in California alone, from a large one in

Los Angeles dubbed Little Tokyo to a tiny section of the farm town of Marysville. After World War II and internment, most of those communities declined or disappeared entirely.

Modern Japanese Americans now delay marriage and have fewer children. They often wed non-Japanese people and identify less strongly with Japanese culture. And they establish places of worship, restaurants, and grocery stores elsewhere. For all those reasons, they may not feel the need to settle in Japantowns, which have become more tourist attractions than actual places to live.

The $595 Meal

Masa, in New York City, is widely believed to be not only the most expensive sushi restaurant in the United States, but the most expensive restaurant of any type!

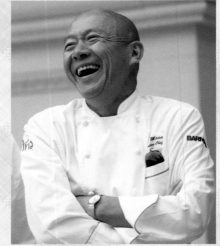

Diners can expect to pay $595 for a sumptuous omakase feast. (Omakase is a Japanese phrase meaning, "I'll leave it up to you," and patrons of Masa allow the famed chef Masayoshi Takayama [right] to choose what they will eat.)

Tax is not included in the quoted $595 price, and things like a beef course or a cup of sake cost extra. Still, diners do at least save some money; tipping is not allowed at Masa, because Takayama believes that hospitality is a bedrock of Japanese culture and should not be dependent on gratuities.

There are now just a handful of significant J-Towns left in the United States, including those in Los Angeles (now shrunk from 120 square blocks to slightly more than 10), San Francisco, and San Jose.

Text-Dependent Questions:

1. What is the Japanese American Citizens League?

2. What happened on December 7, 1941?

3. What is the average life expectancy for Japanese women who follow Japanese government dietary guidelines?

Research Project:

Research what Little Tokyo in Los Angeles was like during its heyday and list the things you would have liked to see, do, and eat there.

RICE AND FISH

Entire books could be written about rice in the Japanese diet. It is even said to be partially responsible for Japan's interconnected, cooperative culture. In American history books, you might read about the concept of "rugged individualism," but that is not a characteristic valued as much in Japan. That's because farming rice requires closely collaborating with your neighbors. Rice is grown in paddies (level fields that are flooded with water), and all the paddies in an area must be flooded and drained at the same time. Additionally, growing rice successfully requires complex irrigation systems, so villagers must get together to collectively pay for and maintain the equipment. So while a single family might be able to plant and harvest a field of wheat by themselves, that doesn't work with rice.

Rice has been cultivated for thousands of years, and until the 19th century, taxes were even paid to the government with rice. There are numerous varieties of rice, including hakumai, *the snowy-white version served with most meals;* genmai, *brown rice that is gaining in popularity because of its health benefits; and* mochigome, *also known as sticky rice, which is often made into sweets.*

Noodles of all types are also popular in Japan. Sometimes these are stir-fried with bits of meat, seafood, and vegetables. Sometimes they are served in broth to make hearty soups. These include udon *noodles made with wheat flour and* soba *noodles made with buckwheat flour.*

If you live in a large city, you may have seen restaurants that specialize in ramen. Ramen is a type of thin egg noodle served in a rich, fatty broth, usually made with pork or chicken. (There are also vegetarian versions.) This can be topped with barbecued meat, bean sprouts, hard-boiled eggs, strips of dried seaweed, and other ingredients to form a warming, flavor-filled meal. (A good bowl of ramen made by a talented cook has little in common with the inexpensive packages of instant ramen that can be found in most American supermarkets!)

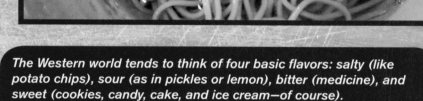

The Western world tends to think of four basic flavors: salty (like potato chips), sour (as in pickles or lemon), bitter (medicine), and sweet (cookies, candy, cake, and ice cream—of course).

In Japan, people recognize a fifth taste called umami, which can be thought of as savory or meaty. It's caused by compounds known as glutamates, which are found in many foods, including soy sauce and aged cheese.

Umami was first described near the start of the 20th century by Kikunae Ikeda, a professor at the Tokyo Imperial University. In 1908, experimenting with kombu seaweed, he identified glutamates as the source of the compelling taste.

SOMETHING FISHY

People in Japan consume much more seafood than those in Western countries. In fact, for more than 1,200 years there was a strong taboo against eating meat in Japan, thanks in large part to Buddhist and Shinto religious influence. That restriction did not end until the 1870s—when an emperor once again took control after centuries of rule by the shogun, and the country became increasingly modernized and Westernized.

Meat is now a larger part of the Japanese diet, but fish of all types is still exceedingly popular. Experts who study food consumption say that the Japanese eat three-quarters of all the tuna caught around the world. (Among the most popular Japanese methods of serving seafood is to make sushi and sashimi.)

Sashimi is thin slices of high-quality raw fish. It is never cooked and it never includes rice.

Sushi, on the other hand is vinegary rice that is mixed with other ingredients—often fish, which accounts for some of the confusion. Sushi can come in the form of norimaki *or rolls. To make* norimaki, *which are common in Japanese restaurants in America, the chosen filling is covered in a thick layer of rice and then rolled in* nori *(seaweed). While raw tuna and salmon are popular fillings for traditional sushi rolls, many Americans enjoy a mild dish that has come to be known as the California roll, filled with avocado, cucumber, and mock crabmeat.*

Although much Japanese food is light and healthful, tempura and katsu could not exactly be described in those terms since they, like kaarage, involve frying foods in oil.

Tempura is a method of dipping foods (especially shrimp and vegetables) in batter, immersing them in bubbling oil until crispy, and serving them with some type of dipping sauce. The Japanese learned the technique from Spanish and Portuguese traders in the 16th century. (The name comes from the Portuguese tempero, *which means "sauce.") Katsu is a thin, breaded cutlet, usually pork or chicken, which was inspired by the schnitzel of Germany and Central Europe.*

Reaching Back

Like members of other ethnic groups that have immigrated, Japanese people sometimes worry about losing their traditions and heritage.

"We gave our son two names, one Western and one Japanese, so that he knows that both cultures are equally important," Sakura explains. "In English, he is called Gryphon, and in Japanese, his name is Tatsu-aki, which means Autumn Dragon." She continues, "I am trying to teach him to speak and read Japanese, although that's hard, since he uses English all day at school, and he prefers the Western-style food that I make for my husband, rather than the traditional foods I prefer."

She realizes that these issues are nothing new. They arose as soon as the Issei first arrived on these shores. Back then, they formed chapters of the Japanese Association of America to maintain links with Japan, to fight discrimination, and to provide social services and cultural activities for members. They opened

Words to Understand

assimilation   the process of taking something in and making it part of what it has joined

Japanese immigrants to the United States represent less than 3 percent of those moving to America from Asia.

Japanese-language schools and community centers. They held public festivals that had the added benefit of introducing their American neighbors to Japanese culture.

For the same reasons that Japantowns have dwindled—intermarriage and **assimilation**—those institutions are slowly becoming things of the past.

Happy Holidays

No matter how much Japanese Americans assimilate, many remain deeply attached to Japanese holidays and the food traditions that go along with them. One example is *Hinamatsuri* (Girl's Day), which is celebrated each year on March 3, when *hishi-mochi* (diamond-shaped rice cakes dyed in spring colors to represent fertility and good health) are served.

 ## To Market, to Market

Although the ingredients needed to make Japanese meals are now widely found in any supermarket, many Japanese people prefer to shop at large Asian markets instead. One of the largest of these is Mitsuwa, whose motto is "Transporting You to the Heart of Japan."

At a Mitsuwa Marketplace, patrons can grab a variety of groceries, eat at one of the many in-store food kiosks, browse a section of Japanese books, take a cooking class, and more.

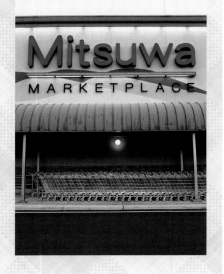

Jubako *boxes filled with delicacies are a key part of New Year celebrations in Japan and among Japanese Americans.*

The most important and beloved of the Japanese holidays is *Oshogatsu* or New Year's Day. In Japan, most businesses close from January 1 to January 3, and families gather to spend time together and eat special treats.

On December 31, it is traditional to eat long noodles as a symbol of long life, and on the following day many families eat elaborate feasts of *osechi ryori*, foods cured in salt or vinegar, or simmered in soy sauce and sake. The prepared pieces of vegetables and fish are tucked into fancy lacquer boxes called *jubako*, and a good chef will make sure to include lucky colors (like pink and white fish cakes), as well as foods with symbolic meaning (like herring roe, which is said to be a sign that the diner will have many children).

Because *osechi ryori* takes so long to prepare, many Japanese people buy ready-made boxes from restaurants.

Lessons Learned

After periods of bigotry and persecution, Japanese Americans are now enthusiastically accepted in the United States, and Japanese food and culture have become widely popular. Japanese consumer brands like Honda, Toyota, Sony, and Panasonic are household names in America; Japanese animation and comic books have influenced those art forms here. And Japanese people have succeeded in every field, from politics (US Senator Daniel Inouye and Congresswoman Patsy Mink, for example), to entertainment (*Star Trek* actor George Takei, who spent years of his childhood in an internment camp), to science (physicist Michio Kaku).

Impact of immigration on jobs

Useful Utensils

Chopsticks originated in China about 5,000 years ago and spread to Japan by 500 CE. According to historians, the very first versions were probably twigs used to retrieve food from cooking pots, but by the time they reached Japan, they were more sophisticated and fashioned from bamboo. (Today chopsticks can be made from a wide variety of materials, from precious metal to plastic.)

The secret to eating with chopsticks is to move only the top one. Keep the bottom stick still while using your first two fingers and thumb to hold the top stick like a pencil, and pinch bits of food between them.

It is considered rude to rest your chopsticks sideways across the top of dishes, spear your food rather than picking it up, suck or lick your chopsticks, pull serving dishes closer with your chopsticks, or point at people or things with them.

While the number of Japanese immigrants now coming to the United States is relatively small compared with the number of Issei who arrived before 1924, there are still some one million people of Japanese descent here now, in every corner of the nation. They've introduced us to their traditions and their foods, but more importantly, they've provided welcome diversity and an example of strength in the face of adversity.

Japanese people bring a wide mix of positive contributions to the United States and to all the countries they move to.

Text-Dependent Questions:

1. What is the mission of the Japanese Association of America?

2. What is a *jubako*?

3. When do Japanese people usually eat *osechi ryori*?

Research Project:

Hinamatsuri and *Oshogatsu* are just two examples of Japanese holidays. Look up others and make a calendar or timeline listing them and describing a little about them. Be creative!

DESSERT

Sugar was not introduced to Japan until the eighth century, when traders brought it from China. Initially, it was used as a medicine, rather than as a sweetener for food. Before then, people cooked with honey and *amazura*, a kind of wild ivy whose leaves produce a sweet liquid.

> *Because the green tea so popular in Japan can be bitter, many people liked to make something sweet to have alongside it, and when tea ceremonies caught on among the ruling classes, a wide variety of Japanese-style treats, called* wagashi, *were developed to accompany the beverage. (Most sweets in Japan are eaten at teatime, rather than at the end of a meal as is done in the West.)*
>
> *Wagashi can be difficult and time-consuming to make at home, so most families buy them from retail candy shops or bakeries. Often the types of* wagashi *on offer correspond to the seasons of the year, so small pink confections molded to look like cherry blossoms are popular in the spring, for example, while those sold in the autumn might mimic brightly colored leaves.*

Among the most popular Japanese desserts is mochi. Strictly speaking, the word refers to sweet rice dough. (To make mochi, short-grain glutinous rice is pounded into a paste and molded into whatever shape the cook desires.) Because it is portable and dense in calories, blocks of mochi were a popular meal for the ancient Japanese warriors known as samurai. Mochi is enjoyed all year long, but is especially associated with the Japanese New Year, since it is considered a symbol of good fortune. Today, when most people in the United States refer to mochi they mean a dessert consisting of a small ball of ice cream wrapped in a thick layer of chewy rice dough. The popular treat was invented by a Japanese American businesswoman named Frances Hashimoto.

During Japan's Edo Period, which spanned from 1603 to 1868, Japanese society was ruled by the Tokugawa military regime (a shogunate). Tai, or sea bream, was a very expensive delicacy, often presented to the shogun as a gift. Even today, some Japanese people hang a picture of tai near the entrance to their homes or shrines, and tai-shaped cakes are given as party favors to wedding guests.

One day, about 100 years ago, as the story goes, a savvy sweet-shop owner wanted to find a way to make his customers think his imagawayaki, round waffle-like cakes stuffed with bean paste, were more special and delicious than those of his competitors. Because tai was considered both a luxury and a symbol of luck, he made a waffle iron that would produce crispy fish-shaped waffles instead of ordinary round ones.

Now, taiyaki, as the treats are called, are sold from street stalls all over Japan, with a variety of flavors and fillings available. They can also be found, premade and frozen, in grocery stores. They are even making a splash in the United States, where one company, Taiyaki NYC, is selling Instagram-worthy fish-shaped cones—although these are stuffed with soft-serve ice cream and toppings rather than bean paste.

RECIPE

Gohan *(Boiled Rice)*
Serves 4
It may seem funny to use a recipe for something as simple as rice, but it's a vital building block of Japanese cuisine, and it should be perfect.

Ingredients:
1 cup Japanese short-grain rice (available at most supermarkets; look in the aisle with other types of rice or in the Asian food aisle)
1¼ cups water (plus more for soaking)

Steps:
Wash the rice and allow it to soak in a saucepan full of water for about 30 minutes.

Drain it using a sieve or colander.

Return the rice to the saucepan, add the water, and bring it to a boil over high heat.

Reduce the heat, cover the pan, and let it simmer until all the water has been absorbed by the rice. This will take about 15-20 minutes.

Fluff with a fork and serve in a bowl.

To eat rice the traditional way, hold the bowl in your left hand, close to your mouth. Use a pair of chopsticks to push the rice into your mouth, slowly rotating the bowl so that you can scoop up every grain.

Find Out More

Books

Andoh, Elizabeth. ***Washoku: Recipes from the Japanese Home Kitchen.*** Berkeley, CA: Ten Speed Press, 2005.

Hosking, Richard and Debra Samuels. ***A Dictionary of Japanese Food: Ingredients and Culture.*** Seattle: Tuttle Publishing, 2015.

Sakamoto, Pamela Rodner. ***Midnight in Broad Daylight: A Japanese American Family Caught Between Two Worlds.*** New York: HarperCollins, 2016.

Websites

https://www.jnto.go.jp/eng/
If you've ever wanted to travel to Japan, you can learn all about the wonderful things there are to do, see, and eat on this site.

http://www.everyculture.com/Ja-Ma/Japan.html
Read about everyday life in Japan and the country's culture here.

https://www.chopstickchronicles.com/
Discover mouthwatering Japanese recipes and beautiful food photos.

Series Glossary of Key Terms

acclimate   to get used to something

assimilate   become part of a different society, country, or group

bigotry   treating the members of a racial or ethnic group with hatred and intolerance

culinary   having to do with the preparing of food

diaspora   a group of people who live outside the area in which they had lived for a long time or in which their ancestors lived

emigrate   leave one's home country to live in another country

exodus   a mass departure of people from one place to another

first-generation American   someone born in the United States whose parents were foreign born

immigrants   those who enter another country intending to stay permanently

naturalize   to gain citizenship, with all its rights and privileges

oppression   a system of forcing people to follow rules or a system that restricts freedoms

presentation   in this series, the style in which food is plated and served

Index

Photo Credits

Australian War Memorial: 38. Dreamstime.com: Americanspirit 8; photographerlondon 9; Leonardo Fontes 18; Lcc54613 20T; Nantarpat Surasingthothong 20B; Ppy2010ha 21T; Emilia420 21B; Ostancov Vladislaw 39; Artit Thongchuea 40; Sergii Koval 42; rawpixelimages 46; Vichai Laorapeepornthong 47; Sirawit Hengthabthim 47; Andrey Armyagov 49T; Hein The 49B; Yosimasa 53; Photowitch 55; Jedimaster 56; Kenishirote 58; Photoraidz 59; Tachjang 60; Kazoka 61. Newscom: Tom Donoghue/Polaris 44. Library of Congress: 14; 23 (Russell Lee); 37 (Ansel Adams). Shutterstock: DnDavis 16; Jazz3311 19; sirtravelot 50; EQRoy 52. Wikimedia Commons: Keno Muneside 7; Viriditas 11; Joe Mabel 12; Leung Cho Pan 24; James Kirkikis 26, 35; Jason Cheng 28; Sirirat Savettanant 30T; Jedimaster 30B; Jamey Elkins 31; Tataya Kudo 32; Reika7 33T; Yasuhiro Armano 33B.

Author Bio

Mari Rich was educated at Lehman College, part of the public City University of New York. As a writer and editor, she has had many years of experience in the fields of university communications and reference publishing, most notably with the highly regarded periodical *Current Biography*, aimed at high school and college readers. She also edited and wrote for *World Authors, Leaders of the Information Age*, and *Nobel Laureates*. Currently, she spends much of her time writing about engineers and engineering.